United in
Prayer &
Worship

mothers | Christian care for
union | families worldwide

United in
Prayer &
Worship

Mothers' Union
Mary Sumner House
24 Tufton Street
London SW1P 3RB
020 7222 5533
email mu@themothersunion.org
www.themothersunion.org

ISBN 0 85943 060 X
fourth print 2002
reprinted 2003

Printed by JW Arrowsmith Ltd, Bristol

Introduction

Throughout the Day

Services and Prayers at Meetings

Prayers and Meditations

Introduction

Welcome to *United in Prayer & Worship*, the new edition of the Mothers' Union Service Book. While we have included some material from the previous edition there are new contributions, a slightly reordered structure and a more detailed index. We have also included suggestions for worship and prayers for many occasions, so that you can adapt and alter these to suit your own needs. We also encourage you to be flexible and open in the way you use this book. It is not intended to restrict you, rather to assist you in the way you offer your service and your prayers to God.

Throughout the Day

Mothers' Union Prayer

Almighty God, our heavenly Father, who gave marriage to be a source of blessing, we thank you for family life, with all its joys and sorrows.

May we know your presence and peace in our homes, fill them with your love and use them to your glory.

Bless all who are married and every parent and child.

Pour out upon us your Holy Spirit, that we may truly love and serve you.

Bless the members of the Mothers' Union throughout the world, unite us in prayer and worship, in love and service, that, strengthened by your grace, we may seek to do your will; through Jesus Christ, our Lord.

Amen

Introduction to Morning Prayers

Gentle God
breathe love within us,
breathe love between us.
From one moment to the next,
you hold us in the palm of your hand.

Morning Prayers

These can be said with or without the Wave of Prayer and you
may wish to use all the text or just some of it.

"UNITED IN PRAYER AND WORSHIP" – from Kenya

PREPARATION

Leader We have come together, the people of God,
drawn by his Spirit, longing for his word,
to praise the holy name of the Lord,
to share the glorious news of grace,
to pray for our needs and the pains of the world,
to rejoice in his love and be sent in his peace.

Leader We are all heirs of the Father

All joint heirs with the Son

Leader renewed in the Spirit

All together we are one.

THE WORD OF GOD

An appropriate verse of Scripture may be said

Leader Lord have mercy

All Lord have mercy

Leader Christ have mercy

All Christ have mercy

continues.............

Leader Lord have mercy
All Lord have mercy
Leader Blessed are those who live in your house
All they will be always singing your praise.
Leader Praise the Lord
All The name of the Lord be praised

Either (a)

Leader The glorious Son of God on high
All is born for us through Mary's womb:
Leader The homeless Prince of Peace on earth
All is crushed and lies in Joseph's tomb
Leader The reigning Lord of life and death
All breaks the bond of time and doom.

Or (b)

Leader Glory to the Father in whom all things began
All Glory to the Son who became the Son of Man,
Glory to the Spirit who inspires and renews.
The Lord our God for ever! Alleluia!

JUBILATE SONG

I will enter his gates with thanksgiving in my heart;
I will enter his courts with praise.
I will say this is the day that the Lord has made;
I will rejoice for he has made me glad.
He has made me glad, he has made me glad;
I will rejoice for he has made me glad.
He has made me glad, he has made me glad;
I will rejoice for he has made me glad.

or any other Song of Praise.

THE SONG OF THE MESSIAH

(Genesis 12.3, Deuteronomy 18.15f, 2 Samuel 7.12f, Isaiah 53.4)

Jesus, the seed of Abraham, blesses the nations;
Jesus, the prophet, like Moses, frees the oppressed:
Jesus, the Lord of King David, leads the people:
Jesus, the Servant of the Lord, suffers and saves:
Jesus, the Son of Man, was crucified and raised.

Leader   Glory to the Father in whom all things began

All   Glory to the Son who became the Son of Man,
Glory to the Spirit who inspires and renews.
The Lord our God for ever! Alleluia!

Or (b)

THE SONG OF JESUS

(Luke 6.27, Matthew 25.35-6, Luke 7.22-23, Luke 10.21)

All   Love your enemies
do good to those who hate you,

Leader   bless those who curse you,
pray for those who abuse you.
I was hungry and you gave me food,
thirsty and you gave me drink,
a stranger and you welcomed me,
naked and you clothed me,
sick and you visited me,
in prison and you came to me.
The blind receive their sight,
the lame walk, the lepers are cleansed.
The deaf hear, the dead are raised:
the good news is preached to the poor
and blessed are those not offended at me.

continues.............

All	Love your enemies
	do good to those who hate you,
Leader	Glory to the Father in whom all things began
All	**Glory to the Son who became the Son of Man,**
	Glory to the Spirit who inspires and renews.
	The Lord our God for ever! Alleluia!

PRAYERS

Leader	United in prayer with our brothers and sisters
	throughout the world, we say together
	The Lord's Prayer
Leader	Show us your mercy, O Lord
All	**and grant us your salvation.**
Leader	O Lord, guide our Queen/President/Prime Minister
All	**and give our leaders wisdom and justice.**
Leader	may your ministers serve you faithfully
All	**and your royal people joyfully.**
Leader	In the valley of the shadow of death;
All	**protect us with your rod and staff.**
Leader	Like trees planted by the waterside;
All	**grant us the fruit of your Spirit.**
Leader	Send us out as the salt of the earth;
All	**and as the light of the world.**
Leader	May the earth be filled with your glory;
All	**as the waters cover the sea.**
Leader	Almighty and everlasting God,
	Father of the Prince of Peace,
	in returning and rest we are saved,
	in quietness and trust is our strength.
	Grant us the blessing of making peace,

and the joy of seeking justice.
Take from our souls the strain and stress,
and let our ordered lives confess,
the beauty of your peace;
through Jesus Christ our Lord. Amen

Prayerful choruses or a hymn may be sung. People may join in
open prayers for contemporary, personal or world needs, or use
some of the following:

The Mothers' Union Prayer

For the Church

Almighty and eternal God,
the only source of power;
grant to all the people of our churches
and our bishops and clergy
your health-giving Spirit of grace;
and that we may truly please you,
pour on us the continual dew of your blessing.
Grant this for the sake of our advocate
and mediator, Jesus Christ. Amen

For mission and evangelism

O God our Father,
give us a passion for your Word
and boldness in telling our neighbour
about your grace.
May the Holy Spirit convict the lost
and draw them to the Saviour,
Jesus Christ our Lord. Amen

For life in towns and cities

Creator God, our heavenly Father,
your Son was a carpenter in Nazareth,
with nowhere to lay his head;
we pray for all those who work paid or unpaid.
Grant them wisdom and honesty, strength and skill,
to provide for themselves
and the needs of our country.
Look with compassion on the poor,
the unemployed and homeless,
the orphans and the hungry,
and grant us your power to work towards justice
in transforming their lives for your glory;
through our risen Lord Jesus Christ. Amen

For guidance

Guide us, Lord, in all we do
with your grace and love,
and grant us your continual help;
that in all our works,
begun, continued and ended in you,
we may glorify your holy name,
and by your mercy attain everlasting life,
through Jesus Christ our Lord. Amen

The Grace...

*This order of service is adapted from "A Service of Morning
Prayer" in "Modern Services" copyright 1991
the Church of the Province of Kenya*

Midday Prayers

The Midday Prayers that are said in the chapel at Mary Sumner House each day, are published every month on the website www.themothersunion.org in the Spirituality section under the heading of 'monthly prayers'.

Midday Prayers in Mary Sumner House usually follow a structure of:

- combined Scriptural passage(s) with a piece of poetry or prose to begin
- a prayer or prayer with responses
- the Wave of Prayer for the month
- the prayer from the Prayer Diary✢ for that day
- intercessions
- optional simple prayers, then 'Bless us now, Lord, in the middle of the day: be with us and with all who are dear to us, and with everyone we meet. Keep us true to you and joyful, simple and loving in all we do. Amen'
- The Grace

✢ the twice yearly Prayer Diary is helpful for using themes to remind everybody of particular needs throughout the year.

Midday Prayers

We beseech you, O Lord, pour your grace into our hearts; that as we have known the incarnation of your Son, Jesus Christ, by the message of an angel, so by his cross and passion we may be brought to the glory of his resurrection; through Jesus Christ our Lord. Amen.

O God, our heavenly Father, we ask you to bless the work of the Mothers' Union throughout the world, and especially in each diocese for which we pray today. *................. Bless our members in their lives and in their homes, that they, being strengthened in love to you and to each other, may serve you faithfully to your glory; through Jesus Christ, our Lord. Amen

continues.............

Blessed Saviour, who at this hour hung upon the cross, stretching forth your loving arms, grant that all people may look to you and be saved; who lives and reigns with the Father and the Holy Spirit, ever one God, world without end. Amen.

O Saviour of the world, who by your cross and precious blood has redeemed us;

Save us and help us, we humbly beseech you, O Lord.

* Every diocese at home and overseas is remembered in turn throughout the year. Details can be found in Worldwide Voices, obtainable from MUe and in each issue of Home & Family.

Afternoon Prayers

These can be said with or without the Wave of Prayer and are suitable for use before an afternoon or evening meeting or conference.

Leader   We have come together to enjoy each other's company and to (learn about.../ hear about.../ discuss.../ plan...)
For many of us the day has been busy:
for some a day packed with happiness and enjoyment;
for others perhaps a day of strain or sadness.
We know we are in the presence of God,
so we are quiet to honour him,
and reflect in silence on what the day has held so far...

The following prayers may be used here, or others from elsewhere in this book, or from your own diocesan resources.

14

For our families and friends

Lord,
we thank you for our families, our friends
and all whom we love.
We bring before you now those dear to us
who need your help or comfort:
those who are ill or in hospital…
those who are in trouble…
All who have difficult decisions to make;
help us to see what we can do for them
and give us the strength and courage to do it;
through Jesus Christ our Lord. Amen

For words – spoken and written

Lord,
we praise you for the gift of words:
the words we hear and read,
the words we speak and write.
As we communicate with others
help us to be sensitive to their circumstances
and responsible in our use of words,
that nothing we say or do
may cause hurt or harm to other people.
We thank you for the gift of your holy Word:
help us to read or listen to it daily,
so that we may learn and understand
more of your great love for us,
and may be able to see both your will for us
and the way to fulfil it.
We ask in the name of Jesus our Saviour. Amen

For our meeting

Lord,
as we meet together,
help us to be aware that we are meeting
not simply with each other, but with you:
make your presence real to each one of us.
Help us to listen, to understand and to remember,
and as we listen, help us to concentrate
so we hear what is intended
and what is your will.
Give us courage to say what needs to be said
and humility to accept decisions
with which we do not agree;
when we finish our meeting,
enable us by your grace,
to go out and fulfil your purpose,
doing what you want us to do;
and to your name be the glory,
through Jesus Christ our Lord. Amen

For God's presence

Lord, when you seem far away, draw near to us;
when we are afraid, lighten our darkness;
when we are down, lift us up;
this we ask in your dear name.

Guildford Diocese, England
"Women at Prayer"

For peace

Creator God,
Maker of all things and giver of life,
have mercy on all the nations of the world.
Send down your abundant peace on every creature.
Let there be calm where there is violence;
peace where there is war;

freedom where there is bondage;
love and unity where there is strife;
abundance of food where there is starvation;
good health where there is sickness;
and life where there is death.
These and other good things we ask of you
through Jesus Christ our Lord.

Mrs J.A. Ibimodi, Kwara Diocese, Nigeria
"Women at Prayer"

Evening Prayers

Leader You, O Lord, are my lamp
All You turn darkness into light

Leader With you, O Lord, is the well of life:
All In your light shall we see light

Leader Your word is a lantern to my feet
All and a light on our path.

Leader Blessed are you, Lord our God, King of the universe!
Your word brings dawn in the morning,
and brings on the dusk at evening,
your wisdom creates both night and day.
You determine the cycles of time,
arrange the succession of seasons,
and establish the stars in their heavenly courses.
Lord of the starry hosts is your name.
Living and eternal God, rule over us always.
Amen

A suitable Psalm or another short reading from Scripture may be read quietly or said here.

Leader   May God, who gives us the light of his grace,
grant that we may come to behold
the light of his glory. Amen

Or   Eternal light, shine into our hearts;
eternal Goodness, deliver us from evil;
eternal power, be our support;
eternal wisdom, scatter the darkness of our ignorance;
eternal pity, have mercy on us;
that with all our heart and mind and strength
we may seek your face
and be brought by your infinite mercy
to your holy presence;
through Jesus Christ our Lord. Amen

Reading(s)

or one of the following or some other

Genesis 1:1-5 Let there be light
Deuteronomy 30:11-20 Choose life
Isaiah 9:2-7 The people who walked in darkness
Isaiah 49: 6b-13 A light to the nations
Isaiah 60: 1-6,19 Your light has come
Luke 2: 29-32 A light to lighten the nations
John 3: 16-21 The Light of the world
John 8: 12-19 The Light of the world
Colossians 1: 13-20 Delivered from darkness
Revelation 22: 1-15 The Lord God will be their light

Kindle, O Lord, in our hearts, we pray,
the flame of that love which never ceases,
that it may burn in us and give light to others.
May we shine for ever in your temple,
set on fire with that eternal light of yours
which puts to flight the darkness of this world
in the name of Jesus Christ your Son our Lord.

St Columba

The Nunc Dimittis

Lord now you let your servant go in peace:
your word has been fulfilled.
My own eyes have seen the salvation:
which you have prepared in the sight of every people;
a light to reveal you to the nations:
and the glory of your people Israel.
Glory to the Father and to the Son:
and to the Holy Spirit;
as it was in the beginning is now:
and shall be forever. Amen

Services and Prayers at Meetings

Suitable for **Branch, Deanery or Diocesan worship**, in church, hall or house. This can be abridged before a meeting as appropriate.

THE PREPARATION
Welcome
Hymn, Psalm or Song
Confession (with/without Absolution)

THE MINISTRY OF THE WORD
Reading
Silence
Hymn, Psalm, Canticle or Scriptural Song (eg.Taize or other)
Reading
Sermon, Talk or Drama
Creed or Affirmation of Faith

THE ACTION *as appropriate*
Baptism, Admission, Commissioning or Presentation,
welcome of specific people; demonstration or appeal.

THE PRAYERS
Intercessions and Thanksgivings
The Lord's Prayer
The Mothers' Union Prayer
The Peace

THE CONCLUSION
Hymn or Song (for collection)
Offertory Prayer
Blessing, Grace and/or Dismissal

The above Service is also suitable for **Communion** and you may
like to add the following post-communion prayer for this purpose.

THE COMMUNION

Post Communion Prayer

> Eternal God
> by this Holy Sacrament you enable us to share in
> your love:
> so bless us and all members of the Mothers' Union
> that, being strengthened in love to you and to
> each other,
> we may serve you faithfully to your glory,
> through Jesus Christ our Lord. Amen.

Canon Frederick Ross,
Vicar of Melbourne, Derbyshire

then conclusion

Special Services

1 SERVICE FOR COMMISSIONING OF OFFICERS

It is customary for officers to be commissioned in church during a diocesan, deanery or parish service appropriate to their area of responsibility.

Minister We have come together here to worship God and to commission .... *(names or eg. "newly elected members")* to office in the Mothers' Union; this is a joyful and important occasion. Each office carries great responsibility, for the Mothers' Union is a worldwide society within the Church, with special concern for all that strengthens and preserves marriage and Christian family life.

.... do you accept office in the Mothers' Union?

Answer I do, the Lord being my helper.

Minister Will you serve God in this way, in the firm belief that the power of the Holy Spirit will guide and direct all who call upon Him?

Answer I will, putting my trust in Him.

Minister *(taking each person in turn by the right hand)*

.... I admit you to the office of

....

in the name of the Father and of the Son and of the Holy Spirit. Amen

When all have been commissioned the priest turns to the congregation and says:

> People of ……………………….................
>
> Will you now welcome your new officer(s)

And there can be a round of applause, or people can offer each other the sign of peace.

Minister will you remember ………………............... in your prayers and give her/him/them your loyal support and encouragement?

Congregation **We will.**

Minister I call on you now to pray that God will bless his servant(s) and provide such gifts and powers as may be needed for the work ahead. Let us pray in silence...

Minister O God,
we ask that you will bless your servants
with a sense of your presence,
and knowledge of your constant love.
Give wisdom and understanding,
your guidance and the humility to accept it.
Grant all members the grace to support
and uphold all who work in your name;
through Jesus Christ our Lord. Amen

O God,
you have called us from many nations and people;
we ask you to bless the work of the Mothers' Union,
and prosper its branches throughout the world.
Give wisdom and courage to those who hold office
and serve on its councils;
unite its members in faith and love,
and grant us your peace in our hearts and homes,
through Jesus Christ our Lord. Amen

The Mothers' Union Prayer

Post-Communion Prayer *suitable for use if the commissioning takes place in a service of Holy Communion.*

> Eternal God
> by this Holy Sacrament you enable us to share
> in your love:
> so bless us and all members of the Mothers' Union
> that, being strengthened in love to you and to
> each other,
> we may serve you faithfully to your glory,
> through Jesus Christ our Lord. Amen

Canon Frederick Ross,
Vicar of Melbourne, Derbyshire

2 MEMBERSHIP SERVICE

This Service is for new members and existing members to affirm and reaffirm their commitments to the Mothers' Union.

To be led by a Minister or Mothers' Union office holder, ideally within Sunday worship but can equally well be used on its own.

Leader   Will the members of the Mothers' Union please stand.

The purpose, Aim and Objects of the Mothers' Union or the current mission statement are read out by a member.

Purpose, Aim and Objects

The purpose of the Mothers' Union is to be specially concerned with all that strengthens and preserves marriage and Christian family life.

The Aim of the Society is the advancement of the Christian religion in the sphere of marriage and family life. In order to carry out its Aim, its **Objects**:

- To uphold Christ's teaching on the nature of marriage and promote its wider understanding.
- To encourage parents to bring up their children in the faith and life of the Church.
- To maintain a worldwide fellowship of Christians united in prayer, worship and service.
- To promote conditions in society favourable to stable family life and the protection of children.
- To help those whose family life has met with adversity.

Leader   Membership of the worldwide Mothers' Union is open to all who have been baptised in the name of the Holy Trinity and who declare support for the Aim and Objects of the Mothers' Union. I ask both new and present members to join in affirming their commitment to the Mothers' Union. Do you reaffirm your baptism promises?

All   I do, with God's help.

Leader   Will you try to uphold and support the Aim and Objects of the Mothers' Union?

All   I will, with God's help.

Leader Will you continue to plan your life to include prayer and Bible reading and worship in Church?

All **I will, by the grace of God.**

Leader (name/s)...
I admit you to membership of the Mothers' Union, in the name of the Father and of the Son and of the Holy Spirit.

The leader greets each new member and they are given their membership card and badge.

If members have moved from another branch/diocese, include the following:

Leader We welcome (name/s)...................................
from..

Leader Members of the Mothers' Union, will you welcome, support and pray for each other?

All **We will, in the power of the Spirit.**

Leader We commit ourselves to the work of Jesus Christ through our membership, saying together the Mothers' Union Prayer:

The Mothers' Union Prayer

Almighty God, our heavenly Father, who gave marriage to be a source of blessing, we thank you for family life, with all its joys and sorrows. May we know your presence and peace in our homes, fill them with your love and use them to your glory. Bless all who are married and every parent and child. Pour out upon us your Holy Spirit, that we may truly love and serve you. Bless the members of the Mothers' Union throughout the world, unite us in prayer and worship, in love and service, that, strengthened by your grace, we may seek to do your will; through Jesus Christ, our Lord. Amen

Prayer for a Branch

Heavenly Father, as members of this branch we commit its life to you, we seek your blessing in all we do; your presence in our fellowship; your inspiration in our activities; your strength in our service to the Church and to the community; help us to be faithful in prayer and worship and outgoing in our witness to the gospel, that we may advance your kingdom, and glorify your name, through Jesus Christ our Lord. Amen

3 NEW BEGINNINGS
– OPENING A NEW GROUP OR BRANCH

As the formation of a new branch is a parish occasion, it should if possible, take place in church. It may include the commissioning of the branch officers and the admission of new members. Before the service the incumbent and members should clarify the aims for the new branch, and draft a Statement of Intent. It may reflect the Aim and Objects of the Mothers' Union or relate specifically to more local needs.

The minister explains to the congregation the history of the formation of the new branch (group), and reads out the Aim and Objects of the Mothers' Union. The minister invites one of the members to read the Statement of Intent on behalf of the new branch.

Minister May the Holy Spirit guide and strengthen you all, that in this, and in all things, you may do God's will in the service of the kingdom of Christ. Amen

Minster In the name of God I commend you to this work, and dedicate the branch to the glory of God.
In the name of the parish of ....
I pledge you our prayers, encouragement and support in the years ahead.

continues.............

Let us pray:
Almighty God,
look with favour upon this branch of the
Mothers' Union;
as the members reaffirm their commitment
to follow Christ and to serve in his name,
give them courage, patience and vision;
strengthen them in their Christian vocation
of witness to the world, and service to others,
through Jesus Christ our Lord. Amen

The Mothers' Union Prayer

*One or more of the following prayers may be used as
appropriate, or a hymn or song may be sung.*

Prayer of commitment *to be said by the members together*

Heavenly Father,
as members of this branch we commit its life to you;
we seek your blessing in all we do:
your presence in our fellowship,
your inspiration in our activities;
your strength in our service to the Church
and to the community;
help us to be faithful in prayer and worship
and outgoing in our witness to the gospel,
that we may advance your kingdom,
and glorify your name,
through Jesus Christ our Lord. Amen

For the leader of the group/branch

Everliving God, strengthen and sustain ....
that with patience and understanding
she may love and care for your people;
grant that under her leadership
the members of the branch may follow Jesus Christ,

offering to you their gifts and talents,
through him who lives and reigns with you and the
Holy Spirit,
one God, now and forever. Amen

For the dedication of a new banner *if appropriate*

We dedicate this banner to the glory of God
in the name of the Father and of the Son
and of the Holy Spirit.
May it be a symbol, visible to all who come to this church,
of our commitment to the advancement of the
Christian religion in the sphere of marriage and
family life.
Father, we also dedicate ourselves,
as individuals and as a branch,
to serve you in following Jesus.
Help us to be faithful in worship, prayer and
Bible reading, and to help others to know your love.
We ask in the name of the same Jesus Christ,
our Lord. Amen

For personal dedication

Father, we dedicate ourselves
to serve you faithfully and to follow Jesus,
to face the future with him,
seeking his special purpose for our lives.
Send us out to work and witness freely,
gratefully and full of hope,
in the power of the Holy Spirit,
and for the honour and glory of your Son,
Jesus Christ our Lord. Amen

The Lord's Prayer

The Grace
and/or **The Blessing**

4 CLOSING A BRANCH OR GROUP

The minister gathers the people together and explains informally the recent history of the branch and the reasons why it is appropriate to bring its existence to an end.

Minister We have come together here to worship God and to thank him for what has been good in the past; this is an important but sad occasion, and we have mixed feelings, but we believe the right decision has been made....

Listen to these words from the Bible:

"Think of the love that the Father has lavished upon us, by letting us be called God's children; and that is what we are...

My dear people, we are already the children of God, but what we are to be in the future has not yet been revealed; all we know is, that when it is revealed we shall be like him because we shall see him as he really is." (1 John 3:1-2)

This is the word of the Lord

All **Thanks be to God.**

The following prayers, or others, can be said by the minister or by members:

Thanksgiving for the past

Ever-loving Father,
we thank you for the work and witness
of the ....branch of the Mothers' Union:
for all by which it is remembered,
for all that it meant to those who belonged to it,
and those who were in any way helped by
its members,
and for everything in its life
which reflected your mercy and love.
We pray for the members who have departed this life,
and for those who have moved away.
We recall the happy times in the past........

For forgiveness

All-merciful Father,
we bring to you for forgiveness all that was amiss
in the life of our branch over the years:
for failing to live up to your gospel:
for the things we were afraid to try,
and those we failed to finish;
for the times when we should have been reaching out
to your people in need but were turned in on ourselves;
for these and other shortcomings
we ask your forgiveness now. Amen

Of hope for the future

We pray for the future of the remaining members:
that they may find comfort and fellowship elsewhere,
may remain true to their membership promises,
and may continue to know your love and power in their
lives.
As we look forward we pray for the life of this parish:
that we may uphold Christ's teaching
on the nature of marriage
and help people to understand and follow it.
That children may be brought up
in the life and faith of the Church,
that family life be honoured and protected,
and that we may provide help
for all whose family life meets with adversity.
This we ask in the name of the same Jesus Christ
our Lord. Amen

The General Thanksgiving *said together*

Almighty God, Father of all mercies,
we your unworthy servants
give you most humble and hearty thanks
for all your goodness and loving kindness.
We thank you for our creation, preservation
and all the blessings of this life;
but above all for your immeasurable love
in the redemption of the world
by our Lord Jesus Christ,
for the means of grace,
and for the hope of glory.
Give us, we pray,
such a sense of all your mercies
that our hearts may be unfeignedly thankful,
and that we show forth your praise,
not only with our lips but in our lives,
by giving up ourselves to your service,
and by walking before you
in holiness and righteousness all our days;
through Jesus Christ,
to whom with you and the Holy Spirit,
be all honour and glory, for ever and ever. Amen

From Common Worship 2000

The Grace

5 A SHORT HEALING SERVICE

OPENING RESPONSES

Leader We come in this service to God,

All **In our need, and bringing with us the needs of the world**

Leader We come to God, who has come to us in Jesus,

All **And who walks with us the road of our world's suffering.**

Leader We come with our faith and with our doubts,

All **We come with our hopes and with our fears.**

Leader We come as we are,
because it is God who invites us to come.

All **And God has promised never to turn us away.**

A song, hymn or psalm may be sung or said. A passage from the Bible may be read, one of the following, or some other.

Psalms 16,23,46,103,142

Mark 1:29-45, Mark 2:1-12, Mark 9:14-29

Luke 7:18-29, Luke 11:5-13, John 5:1-15

John 14:12-17, Acts 3:1-16, 2 Corinthians 12:7-10

PRAYERS OF INTERCESSION
One or more of the following may be used, followed by the names of people for whom healing is asked.

O Jesus, you who walk with the wounded
along the road of our world's suffering,
we seek your grace of healing
for the broken people and places of our world:

continues.............

33

O God, open to us today the sea of your mercy
and water us with full streams,
from the riches of your grace
and springs of your kindness.
Make us children of quietness and heirs of peace:
kindle in us the fire of your love;
strengthen our weakness by your power
and bind us closer to you and to each other.

We bring to God someone whom we remember today,
and for whom we want to pray...
We bring to God someone who is hurting today
and needs our prayer...
We bring to God a troubled situation in our
world today...
we bring to God anyone whom we find hard
to forgive or trust...
We bring ourselves to God
that we might grow in generosity of spirit,
clarity of mind,
and warmth of affection. Amen

Leader   Jesus said "Come to me all who are troubled and
I will give you rest".
So come,
you who are burdened by regrets and anxieties,
you who are broken in body or spirit,
you who are torn by relationships and by doubt,
you who feel deeply within yourselves
the divisions and injustices of our world.
Come,
for Jesus invites us to bring him all brokeness.

*Those who want to make special prayers either for themselves or
for someone else, or for the needs of the world, can be invited to
come forward, and kneel or stand. Those who wish to share in
the laying on of hands may come and simply place a hand on the
shoulder of the person in front of them.*

O great God, grant us your light.
O great God, grant us your grace.
O great God, grant us your joy
and let us be made pure in the well of your health.

Spirit of the living God, present with us here,
enter you now, body, mind and spirit,
and heal you of all that harms you,
in Jesus' name. Amen

God to enfold you.
Christ to touch you.
The Spirit to surround you. Amen

May the healing touch of Jesus
the love of God the Father
and the power of Holy Spirit
be upon you to cleanse, comfort and strengthen you
and to give you peace. Amen

CLOSING PRAYER

Leader   And now may the God of hope fill us with all joy and peace in believing, that we may abound in hope in the power of the Holy Spirit. Amen

This service is adapted from "A Service of Prayer for Healing" in the Iona Community Worship Book, copyright 1991 The Iona Community, Glasgow G51 3UU Scotland

SERVICES & PRAYERS AT MEETINGS • HEALING

PRAYERS FOR BRANCH, GROUP OR HOUSE MEETINGS

The following prayers can be used for any meeting whether large or small.

Leader God has promised us that when two or three are gathered together in his name, he will be there among them, so we pray:

Either a)

Holy God,
help us to draw near to you in this time of prayer,
that we may worship you with all our hearts,
with all our minds, and with all our strength,
and that we may love and serve our neighbours in
everything we do. Amen

Or b)

The Lord is faithful to all his promises
and loving towards all he has made.
The Lord upholds all those who fall
and lifts up all who are bowed down.
The Lord is near to all who call upon his name,
to all who call on him in truth.
He fulfils the desires of those who ask him,
he hears their cry and saves them.

adapted from Psalm 145

Let us pray for unity of all peoples on this earth in the words our Saviour taught us:

The Lord's Prayer

For today's meeting

Jesus, our Saviour:
you knew the pain of hard work and long hours
both in Nazareth and in your ministry with your
disciples;

renew us now in our meeting here:
help us to hear other people's points of view,
and to discern your will as we make decisions;
grant us vision, discernment, courage and generosity.
When our meeting is over,
give patience and loyalty to all who disagree,
discretion about what has been discussed,
and diligence to those who have to carry out
what has been decided. Amen

For the coming of the kingdom

Holy Spirit of God,
fill us with your power,
that in all we do and say,
we may show forth the love of God,
and proclaim the good news of the kingdom
to the peoples of the world;
we ask in the name of Jesus Christ,
our Lord and Saviour. Amen

PRAYERS FOR DEANERY, DIOCESAN COUNCIL OR WORLD WIDE COUNCIL MEETINGS

O Lord our God, listening to us here,
you accept also the prayers of our sisters and brothers
in Africa, Asia, the Pacific, the Americas and Europe,
we are all one in prayer.
So may we, as one, rightly carry out your commission
to witness and to love in the Church
and throughout the world.
Accept our prayers graciously,
as we offer them in Jesus' name. Amen

God of all who journey,
we thank you for bringing us safely to this place.
We thank you for this opportunity of worshipping
together.

continues.............

You have brought us here from different
geographical points,
different theological points and from different points
of experience.
We pray that your Spirit will guide us (this
morning/today/throughout this Council/Conference)
to journey together across the boundaries that divide us:
the boundaries that we fear,
the boundaries that enthuse and excite us
but which demand that we take risks.
Bless us as we are gathered here with you
and allow us to proclaim your kingdom;
we ask in Jesus' name. Amen

Revd Janice Jones, Bangor

Lord God, we dedicate ourselves
to serve you faithfully
and to follow Christ.
Send us out to work and witness freely,
gratefully and hopefully,
in the power of the Holy Spirit,
and for the honour and glory of your Son, Jesus Christ.
Amen

PRAYERS FOR COMMITTEE MEETINGS

Faithful God,
we thank you for the privilege of meeting
together today,
for the support and strength we give to each other
on this day,
for the happiness, encouragement and inspiration
we share in our time together.

Guide us as we speak,
and when we listen,
in all our talking, our thinking, our planning
and our deciding,
may we discern your will more clearly.
May we work towards your purpose for us,
so that our hearts will be open to one another,
with compassion and consideration.
When we meet together, you are always among us,
meet with us now as we offer this day to your glory.
Amen

Loving God,
we come here today recognising once again
that you have called us to your service.
Each one of us is unique and so our service to you
is unique,
let us celebrate our unique gifts at this meeting.
Let our different roles and ministries be a source of
strength to us,
a source of diversity within unity.
Guide us therefore, as we meet now,
all with something to offer and something to receive,
as we consider the past and plan for the future,
let our hearts and minds be open to you and to each
other.
We thank you for all that has been accomplished in and
through the Mothers' Union, and we pray that you will
enable us in our different ways, to build for the future
in love and service to your greater glory.
Through Jesus Christ our Lord.
Amen

Prayers and Meditations

THE CYCLE OF PRAYER

The cycle of prayer is part of the Mothers' Union calendar. It highlights key days in the year that are of significance to us. You may find using some of these days helpful for focussing on a theme or for drawing people's attention to different aspects of our work. There are also suggested Biblical texts for each day.

Dates for the Cycle of Prayer, other than those which are international days or celebration days within the Mothers' Union, are linked with UK dates. These should be adapted and added to, for local days of prayer. As some of these dates change from year to year, please check either on the Spirituality pages of the Website: www.themothersunion.org or by contacting the Prayer & Spirituality Unit.

Suggested Bible readings, prayers and meditations

January – Week for Christian Unity

Ephesians 4. 13-16

> Lord God, we thank you
> for calling us into the company of those
> who trust in Christ and seek to do his will.
> May your Spirit guide and strengthen us
> in mission and service to your world;
> for we are strangers no longer
> but pilgrims together on the way to your kingdom.

Prayer of the Inter-Church Process
– The Swanwick Declaration

February – Celebrating Marriage

In the week of St Valentine's Day

Mark 10. 6-9; Roms 12. 9-13; 1 Corinthians 13; Ephesians 5.21-end

> Loving, everlasting God,
> we do well, always and everywhere to give you thanks.
> You created us in love to share your divine life.
> We see our high destiny in the love of husband and
> wife which bear the imprint of your own love. Love is
> our origin, love is our constant calling; love is our
> fulfilment in heaven. The love of man and woman is
> made holy in the sacrament of marriage and becomes
> the mirror of your everlasting love. Amen

MU Australia

March (first Friday) – World Day of Prayer

Women's World Day of Prayer in UK and some other countries

Luke 14. 15-24

> Lord, you invite us – not some of us,
> all of us;
> not the good and righteous,
> all of us – unconditionally

> Lord we come –
> meeting you,
> meeting each other,
> accepting each other,
> unconditionally.

We rejoice in the great variety of humanity, that we come from different races, cultures and traditions and have various gifts.

We rejoice that you call each one of us to fullness of life and in the diversity of people who have responded to your call.

We rejoice in the power of your love to bind all together in one, and in being together in this service and in sharing in fellowship across the world.

We rejoice in the place of our World Day of Prayer

...........................as a movement carried on by women;

....................as a spark in so many ecumenical ventures

...............................in its present place alongside other movements towards unity.

We come and rejoice. Amen

From the Centenary World Day of Prayer Service 1987,
WWDP in England, Wales & Northern Ireland

March/April

Lent

Matthew 4.1-11; Mark 1.12-13; Luke 4. 1-13

> Almighty and everlasting God, who hatest nothing that thou hast made, and dost forgive the sins of all them that are penitent:
> Create and make in us new and contrite hearts, that we worthily lamenting our sins, and acknowledging our wretchedness, may obtain of thee, the God of all mercy, perfect remission and forgiveness; through Jesus Christ our Lord. Amen

> *Collect for Ash Wednesday – Book of Common Prayer*

Mothering Sunday (4th Sunday of Lent)

Luke 2. 41-52

> **A Mother's Prayer**
> Creator God, I thank you for the privilege of bringing children into this world and for the gift of new life. Give me your guidance, your love, your strength, on each new day I share with you the nurturing and care of my family, may they grow in stature and in knowledge of you, filled with your wisdom and your joy of living.

> *MU New Zealand*

Lady Day – 25th March *unless moved by early Easter date*

Luke 1.26-38

> O Lord Jesus Christ
> give us, we pray, the graces of Mary;
> faith, patience, ready obedience,
> thankfulness and courage.
> As Mary said 'My soul proclaims the greatness of the Lord,
> and my spirit rejoices in God my Saviour'

continues.............

43

so give us the gift of thankfulness and joy.
As Mary 'kept all these sayings in her heart'
so may we be faithful in hearing and reflecting
on your Word.
As Mary said 'Do whatever he tells you'
grant us readiness to do the work to which we
are called.
As Mary stood by the cross
grant that we may never be ashamed to confess you
as our crucified and risen Saviour. Amen

The Mothers' Union Worship Book

Easter

Matthew 28.1-10; Mark 16.1-10; Luke 24.1-12; John 20.1-10

God Almighty
we praise your holy name in this joyful Eastertide.
We thank you, Lord,
because through your death and resurrection
we have won the victory and your redeeming grace
and love.
Loving Father God, fill us with new life
so that we may love one another
and do what you want us to do
in sharing your love with those who do not know you,
in Jesus' name we pray. Amen

Aipo Rongo Mothers' Union, Papua New Guinea

Vocations Sunday

Micah 6.8; Rom 12.1-13; 1Cor 12.4-13

> God has created me
> to do him some definite service:
> he has committed some work to me
> which he has not committed to another.
> I have my mission –
> I may never know it in this life,
> but I shall be told it in the next.
> Somehow I am necessary for his purposes:
> as necessary in my place
> as an Archangel in his.
> I have a part in this great work;
> I am a link in a chain,
> a bond of connection between persons.
> He has not created me for nothing.
> I shall do good, I shall do his work;
> I shall be an angel of peace,
> a preacher of truth in my own place.
> Deign to fulfil your high purposes in me.
> I am here to serve you, to be yours,
> to be your instrument.

From Cardinal Newman

May – Members' Day many members visit Mary Sumner House

See Members' Week – August

June (first Saturday)
International Day of Prayer against violence against children

Matthew 19.13-15; Mark 10.13-16; Luke 18.15-17
Matthew 18.1-6; Mark 18.36-42

> Lord, we cry out to you today for the children of our world who are at risk. For those who are abused and exploited; for those who have been orphaned by war or as a result of AIDS. Lord be their comforter. Bless those who reach out and care for them. Amen

Wakefield Diocese

Celebrating Father's Day
In some areas Father's Day is celebrated on June 29th, Feast of St Peter and St Paul.

Psalm 103.13; Matthew 7.8-11

A Father's Day Prayer

Thank you, friend Jesus,
for my father who loves me,
for my grandfather who cares for me,
and for God, your father and mine,
who made me and is always with me.

How lucky I am!

Gaynell Bordes Cronin

August
Mary Sumner Day – 9th August

Proverbs 31.26-31

> Lord, we give thanks for the life of Mary Sumner, for
> her obedience to your calling, for her vision for the
> Mothers' Union. We pray that through the grace of your
> Holy Spirit we may receive renewed confidence and
> share that vision. We give you thanks and praise for
> the many people around the world who reach out in the
> name of the Mothers' Union. Through our work may we
> touch the lives of those we meet, that they, too, may
> know your love. Amen

Members' Week

2 Corinthians 3.18

> Christ has no body now on earth but yours,
> no hands but yours,
> no feet but yours.
> Yours are the eyes through which he must look out
> Christ's compassion on the world.
> Yours are the feet with which he is to go about
> doing good,
> yours are the hands with which he blesses now.

St Teresa of Avila

October – National Parents' Week

Matthew 18.10

> Lord of all, we give thanks for the work of Mothers'
> Union members in supporting families around the
> world. We ask that all children may be loved, respected
> and nurtured by those who care for them.

Mothers' Union

November
All Saints – 1st November

2 Cor 6.16b+7.1; Heb 12.22-24a

Ephesians 1.17-19

"May the God of our Lord Jesus Christ, the Father of
glory, give you a spirit of wisdom and perception of
what is revealed, to bring you to full knowledge of him.
May he enlighten the eyes of your mind, so that you
can see what hope his call holds for you, how rich is
the glory of the heritage he offers among his holy
people, and how extraordinarily great is the power that
he has exercised for us believers..."

Being Part of the Whole

1 Corinthians 12.12-20

A meditation

In the silence of early morning,
broken only by the ticking of the clock,
somewhere
someone is dying,
a baby is born,
people sleep under comfortable duvets,
others wake stretching
cold cramped limbs
under musty cardboard.
Some will meet the day with joy
others with sadness and mourning.
Some will eat plenty,
others have little or nothing.
Some will walk in freedom,
children playing without fear,
others live with
the sound of firing
and crying in their ears.

In the silence
of early morning
I think briefly
of our worldwide family,
but, Lord,
you think of all of us
all of the time.

Diocese of Newcastle, England

O God, who has bound us together in this bundle of life, give us grace to understand how our lives depend on the courage, industry, honesty and integrity of each other. May we be mindful of the needs of others, grateful for the faithfulness one to another, and faithful in our responsibilities to each other; through Jesus Christ our Lord. Amen

International Day against Violence against Women – 25th November

Matthew 10.26-31; Luke 12.1-6

Lord,
we pray for the women of the world
so often victims
of uncaring governments
of unseen forces which exploit
and use and keep them poor
victims of poverty and hunger
of abuse, maltreatment and commercialisation.

Lord,
may they be conscious
that you are struggling with them
that you are sharing their pain
and understanding their emotions and frustrations
that you are with them and for them

continues.............

Lord,
help them to understand
that your love is strong
that your love is able to defeat all those powers
seen and unseen which are ranged against them.

Lord,
you are the Living God, the Lord of resurrection,
empower us all
to be prepared to stand up and be counted
to be constantly alive
to become new and effective persons
to trust in you and rely on your promises
to unite us with women the world over in the
bond of love.

From Suffering Women by Revd Mair Bowen,
Women's World Day of Prayer 2000

December – Advent

Matthew 3.1-11; Matthew 24.36-44, Matthew 25.1-13;
Mark 1.1-8; Luke 3.1-16

**Lord, in this holy season of Advent, our thoughts
turn to the coming of the Christ-child and to Mary
the mother-to-be.**
We remember the journey taken by the Holy Family and
we ask that as we journey through life, we may show
the same love, care and obedience to God's will.

Give us ever thankful hearts, filled with compassion
and understanding, that we may in return, share these
gifts with others. Amen

Manchester Diocese

Christmas

Matthew 8.18-24; Luke 2.1-7; John 1.1-14, John 3.16

> Come, O long-expected Jesus, born to set your
> people free;
> born your people to deliver; born a child and
> yet a king;
> born to reign in us for ever; now your gracious
> kingdom bring.

Charles Wesley

PRAYERS ROUND THE YEAR

*This outline allows for the leader to include variable Bible readings
and prayers, appropriate to the day, season or chosen theme.
A seasonal or thematic introductory sentence may be used.*

Leader   O worship the Lord in the beauty of the holiness

All   **Let the whole earth stand in awe of him**

Leader   God is Spirit

All   **They that worship him must worship him in spirit
and in truth**

Leader   Through our weakness and ineffectiveness
we hinder the coming of God's kingdom.
Let us ask for pardon and forgiveness, saying together

All   **O most merciful Father,
we confess that we have done little
to forward your kingdom and to advance your
glory.
Forgive our failures, pardon our shortcomings
and give us greater zeal in your service,
for Jesus Christ's sake. Amen**

BIBLE READING appropriate to the theme or season

THE COLLECT OF THE DAY or other appropriate prayer

INTERCESSIONS

Led by the Leader, or others, or open prayer. After each prayer these words may be said or sung:

> O Lord hear my prayer, O Lord hear my prayer,
> when I call, answer me.
> O Lord hear my prayer, O Lord hear my prayer,
> come and listen to me.

Ateliers et Presses de Taize 71250
Taize communaute, France

A SEASONAL HYMN OR SONG may be sung

Leader   To end our time of prayer let us say together

The Lord's Prayer

The Mothers' Union Prayer

The Grace

PRAYER AND THANKSGIVING – A BASIC STRUCTURE

Leader   Let us come into the presence of the Lord,
in the silence of our hearts
we come to you our Lord and God.

All   **The Mothers' Union Prayer**

        or Mary Sumner's Personal Prayer

        Glory to the Father....

or   **Glory be to the Father....**

Specific intercessions and thanksgiving should be offered here.
These may begin with:

Today's meeting, concerns, specific requests, petitions

or news items (local/national/international).

and/or current issues in the Church such as:
the sick, bereaved, the lonely, victims of crime, the unemployed,
the marginalised, the dispossessed, the hungry, the persecuted,
refugees and victims of war, for justice, peace, fellowship of
God's people, Church leaders, Church partnerships in world
mission and in ecumenism,

or you can use the prayer for today from the *Prayer Diary*.

Leader   The stone which the builders have rejected has
become the corner stone

All   **The stone which the builders have rejected has
become the corner stone.**

Leader   Like living stones we build our spiritual home

All   **Like living stones we build our spiritual home**

Leader   Christ our light and our hope, as we build our spiritual
homes today, give us all that we need to become living
stones, to become corner stones wherever we work
for your greater glory.
Through Christ our Lord. Amen

PRAYERS & MEDITATIONS • THANKSGIVING

PRAYERS FOR SPECIAL TIMES

Prayers at Times of Adversity

The Lord is near. Do not be anxious about anything, but in everything, by prayer and petition with thanksgiving, make your requests known to God. And the peace of God, which passes all understanding, will keep your hearts and minds in Christ Jesus. (Philippians 4:5-7)

A selection should be made from the following prayers, to suit the occasion and the people's concerns, with the addition of hymns or songs, Bible reading or other appropriate prayers.

The Love of God

Leader What can separate us from the love of God?
Can sickness or death?

All **No nothing can separate us from the love of God**

Leader Can danger or war?

All **No nothing can separate us from the love of God**

Leader Can sadness or despair?

All **No nothing can separate us from the love of God**

Leader Can the nuclear bomb or the end of the world?

All **No nothing can separate us from the love of God**

Leader Can failure or rejection?

All **No nothing can separate us from the love of God**

Leader Can loneliness or fear?

All **No nothing can separate us from the love of God**

David Adam from "The Edge of Glory" Triangle/SPCK
Holy Trinity Church, Marylebone Rd, London NW1 4DU

For God's will on earth

Leader   Let us ask God for the coming of his kingdom:

        O God, into the pain of the tortured

All   **breathe stillness**

Leader   Into the hunger of the very poor

All   **breathe fullness**

Leader   Into the wounds of our planet

All   **breathe wellbeing**

Leader   Into the deaths of your creatures

All   **breathe life**

Leader   Into those who long for you

All   **breathe yourself**

Leader   Your kingdom come, your will be done

All   **The kingdom, the power and the glory are yours,
now and for ever. Amen**

For people in need *as appropriate*

Leader   We bring (name) in weakness

All   **For your strengthening**

Leader   We bring (name) in sickness

All   **For your healing**

Leader   We bring (name) in trouble

All   **For your calming**

Leader   We bring (name) in pain

All   **For your comfort**

Leader   We bring (name) who is lost

All   **For your guidance**

Leader   We bring (name) who is lonely

continues.............

All	For your love
Leader	We bring (name) who is dying
All	For your resurrection

Father us surround
Every foe confound
    Jesus entwine
    Keep us thine
Spirit enfold
In thy hold
    Sacred three enthrall
    To thee we call.

David Adam from "The Edge of Glory" Triangle/SPCK
Holy Trinity Church, Marylebone Rd, London NW1 4DU

For those in prison

Merciful Father,
be with those in prison who have offended against
the law;
may they come to know your love and forgiveness,
and turn to you in true repentance,
that they may have hope for the future
and the opportunity of making a fresh start.

Lord,
be with all political prisoners;
grant that they will not feel forgotten by the world
at large;
give them courage and hope in their ordeal,
and help them according to their needs,
through Jesus Christ, our Lord. Amen

Freda Howes, Winchester Dicoese
"Women at Prayer"

Prayer for all who live shattered lives

Lord, we are a broken people,
broken through pain, fear and doubt.
Your broken body, broken for us on the cross
and in the breaking of the bread in Eucharist,
is your great act of love for us.
So we ask you,
take our shattered lives and make them whole,
melt our hearts, transform our thoughts,
that we may accept each moment as it comes to us,
with faith and trust, a simple 'I will it Lord,'
that all that happens has your seal upon it,
and with our life,
we will complete our way. Amen

For renewal

With great power the apostles gave their testimony to
the resurrection of the Lord Jesus, and great grace
was upon them. (Acts 4:3)

Reading Psalm 96

*Pause for silent thought especially on the glory of God, his
generosity to his people, and our individual response.*

*Pause for silent thought, especially to discover what keeps each
one of us from telling people the good news of Jesus Christ.*

Reading John 20:21-22

Leader We ask for forgiveness,
and ask that the Holy Spirit will come upon us
dispel all our fears, and strengthen us.
We pray that we may be drawn to those who need you,
Lord Jesus Christ. That we may be able to make them
your disciples and teach them your commands:
Lord in your mercy

All **Hear our prayer**

Reading Matthew 28:16-end

INTERCESSION

Leader Lord,
we pray for renewal in the Church,
we offer to you our own faith and love,
and our readiness to hold to you, come what may;
we offer our faith in the saving love of Jesus;
we offer our faith in the Holy Spirit,
present and active in the world,
in the hearts and minds of those
who do not yet recognise the love of Christ;
we offer ourselves as instruments of evangelism:
Lord in your mercy

All **Hear our prayer**

Pause for silent or open prayer

Leader Heavenly Father
by his death and resurrection your Son, Jesus Christ
won the victory over sin and death, and set us free.
Grant us joy in believing now,
and grace both to rejoice with those who rejoice,
giving glory to you,
and to weep with those who weep,
sharing with them the good news
of your comforting presence,
and the hope of salvation through Jesus Christ our
Lord. Amen

Almighty God,
you called your Church to bear witness
that you were in Christ
reconciling the world to yourself:
help us to proclaim the good news of your love,

that all who hear it may be drawn to you;
through him who was lifted up on the cross
and reigns with you in the union of the Holy Spirit,
one God, now and forever. Amen

Collect for Trinity 13 – Common Worship 2000

Prayer for Stewardship of God's Creation

If the Earth were only a few feet in diameter

If the Earth were only a few feet in diameter, floating a few feet above a field somewhere, people would come from everywhere to marvel at it. People would walk around it, marvelling at its big pools of water, its little pools and the water flowing between the pools. People would marvel at the bumps on it, and the holes in it, and they would marvel at the very thin layer of gas surrounding it and the water suspended in the gas. The people would marvel at all the creatures walking around the surface of the ball, and at the creatures in the water. The people would declare it as sacred because it was the only one, and they would protect it so that it would not be hurt. The ball would be the greatest wonder known, and people would come to behold it, to be healed, to gain knowledge, to know beauty and to wonder how it could be. People would come to love it, and defend it with their lives, because they would somehow know that their lives, their own roundness, could be nothing without it. If the Earth were only a few feet in diameter.

Source unknown

A Prayer for the New Year

God bless our year
giving us time for the task,
peace for the pathway
wisdom for the work
friends for the fireside
love to the last.

The Mothers' Union Anthology of Public Prayer

MEDITATIONS

What does love look like?

It has the hands to help others.
It has the feet to hasten to the poor and needy.
It has the eyes to see misery and want.
It has the ears to hear the sighs and sorrows of men.
That is what love looks like.

St Augustine of Hippo

I imagine...

I imagine myself to be in the presence of Christ
I reveal myself to Christ's presence in silence...
For it forgives... heals... creates.

There are many things within me that are unworthy...
I keep silent when I should speak out...
I turn my eyes away from the unlovely...
I fail to lift my hands to reach the lost...
My ears are closed to cries of pain...
My feet walk my own way and not the way of God.

Which of these things would Jesus have me
change today?

And I hear Jesus say –
'As far as my love for you is concerned,
whether you change or not,
my love for you is unconditional.'

And I reply –
'Jesus, what would you
have me change today?'

Now I see Christ's new life flooding into me.

Finally I rest in his loving presence.

Prayers of Intercessions with times for silence

*This worship outline provides for long periods of quiet during
which everyone can concentrate on the particular subject for
which prayers are being offered, and if they wish say their
prayers aloud. The Leader can then collect up all the prayers,
both spoken and unspoken, by saying "Lord in your mercy". An
appropriate verse of the Bible, or sentence, could be used at the
beginning or a quiet hymn or song can be sung.*

Leader   Let us sit quietly for a while and draw away from all the
busy things which have been occupying us, looking
instead to our Father...

**Leader
or All**   Drop thy still dews of quietness
till all our strivings cease
take from our souls the strain and stress
and let our ordered lives confess
the beauty of thy peace.

Leader   O Lord our Father, we come into your presence
with awe;
we thank you that we shall be received with love.
Amen

Time of quiet

Leader Your love and holiness remind us of our unholiness.
We acknowledge the times when we have made you
sad by our actions and thoughts.
We ask you to forgive us our times of laziness...
bad temper... selfishness... unkindness...
impatience... disobedience...
and other sins which we and you know about...
We ask in silence for your forgiveness.

Time of quiet

Leader Merciful Lord,
Grant your people grace to withstand the temptations
of the world, the flesh and the devil, and with pure
hearts and minds to follow you the only God; through
Jesus Christ our Lord. Amen

Post Communion prayer,
Third Sunday of Lent, Common Worship

Leader We remember, God, with thanks for the times recently
when we have been very aware of your generosity to us.
We name them now...

Time of quiet

Leader Lord in your mercy
All **Hear our prayer**

Leader Lord Jesus, we bring them to you now, for your healing
touch, those whom we know who are ill, at home or in
hospital, and all who love and care for them...

Time of quiet

Leader Lord in your mercy
All **Hear our prayer**

Leader We pray for those who are in trouble, or need of other
kinds...

Time of quiet

Leader Lord in your mercy
All **Hear our prayer**

Leader Father in heaven,
we, your children, bring before you our families,
and the children for whom we are responsible
as parents, godparents, or grandparents,
and as members of your Church in this place...

Time of quiet

Leader Lord in your mercy
All **Hear our prayer**

Leader Almighty God, we pray for the needs of this parish...

Time of quiet

Leader Lord in your mercy
All **Hear our prayer**

Leader God of all,
we pray for the needs of the world,
and especially for peace and justice...

Time of quiet

Leader Lord in your mercy
All **Hear our prayer**

continues.............

63

PRAYERS & MEDITATIONS • INTERCESSIONS

Leader   Finally we pray for the Mothers' Union here
and throughout the world, for family life
and for all who are married, widowed, single or in
relationships, as we say together

The Mothers' Union Prayer

Leader   O Lord, our loving God,
we ask you to keep us, and those for whom we have
prayed,
close to yourself,
that we may find in your love our strength and peace.
Amen

from Margaret Hopkins, Peterborough Diocese

This time of intercession may finish with the **Grace**

FAMILY LIFE PRAYERS AND INTERCESSIONS

Prayers of Intercession

These or other simple prayers are said by the leader, or by older children, or by a family together

For mothers

Lord Jesus,
as your mother Mary cared for you
throughout your earthly life,
so may all mothers care for their children,
giving comfort and courage, praise and advice,
sharing laughter and tears.
Help them to be patient and understanding:
to know when to act and when to stand back,
so that their children may grow up
to know your love and presence in their lives.
Lord Jesus, hear our prayer.

For family life

Father in heaven,
we pray for the homes and family life
of all who are here today:
help us to care for each other
and to take the trouble both
to talk and to listen to each other.
Help us not only to forgive and forget,
but also to be willing to apologise
and to receive forgiveness.
We pray in the name of Jesus Christ, our Redeemer.

For those whose family life is difficult

Father we pray for all unhappy families;
give healing where children or parents are ill
or in hospital;
strengthen mothers and fathers
who cannot provide for their children;
give comfort where parents are separated
or children have run away or are in trouble;
be with all who are alone or lonely;
we ask in the name of Jesus.

For the Church

Almighty God,
we pray for the family of the Church;
that all Christians may work together in harmony
for the spread of the Gospel of Jesus Christ.
and the building up of your peace.

For the World

O God, the Father of us all,
direct our leaders of the world that all your children
may live together in justice and in peace.
We pray that fighting and war may come to an end.
We pray particularly for .....

Leader   As our Saviour Jesus Christ has taught us
so we say together the Family prayer

All   The Lord's Prayer, the Grace

Prayer for peace

Almighty and everlasting God,
let justice and peace embrace our lands,
let love and security replace violence and pain,
let hands raised in anger and hands ready to strike,
become hands ready to offer peace.

We dream of a time when fear becomes faith,
when love and respect walk side by side,
when all people see the world, as if through Your eyes:
and recognise each other as God's own children.
We pray for a time when the weapons of destruction
and the desire for power,
become dreams of justice, equality and freedom,
and that these dreams become reality.

May ours be the eyes that see the poverty in our world
may ours be the ears that hear the cries of your people
May ours be the hands that work for transformation
to bring about your kingdom on this earth.
Great God of power, this is our prayer. Amen

O God, when we turn from you we fall
when we turn to you we rise,
when we stand with you we shall live forever;
grant us your help in all our duties,
your guidance in all our perplexities,
and your peace in all our sorrows,
through Jesus Christ our Lord. Amen

adapted from St Augustine of Hippo

ARROW PRAYERS

- How great is your name, O Lord, our God.

- Watch over my loved ones this day, O Lord, and keep them safe.

- Give me the courage, O God, to face and to cope with this difficult situation.

- Lord, teach me how important it is to be gentle.

- Lord, listen to my cry, for I am in the depths of despair. Psalm 142.6

- Lord, bring justice to our world. That your people may live in the joy of your peace.

- Lord, teach me to listen to my body...to know when to rest.

- Show me this day, O Lord, what you would have me do for you.

- Lord be with me and within me.

- Calm me, Lord, as you still the storm.

- Lord have mercy.

- Lord, give peace to our troubled world.

- I praise and thank you, Lord, for your goodness to me. Stay always close to me.

MU Australia

The Indoor Members' Prayer

O God, our heavenly Father,
our strength and peace and joy,
bless all who are Indoor Members.

Give us your grace
according to our need;
help us to know and love
and trust you more,
to pray better and always to
do your will;
through Jesus Christ, our Lord. Amen

The Lord's Prayer

a) Our Father in heaven, hallowed be your name, your
kingdom come, your will be done, on earth as in
heaven. Give us today our daily bread. Forgive us our
sins as we forgive those who sin against us. Lead us
not into temptation but deliver us from evil. For the
kingdom, the power, and the glory, are yours now and
for ever. Amen

b) Our Father, who art in heaven, hallowed be thy name;
thy kingdom come; thy will be done; on earth as it is in
heaven. Give us this day our daily bread. And forgive
us our trespasses, as we forgive those who trespass
against us. And lead us not into temptation; but deliver
us from evil. For thine is the kingdom, the power and
the glory, for ever and ever. Amen

The Apostles' Creed

I believe in God, the Father almighty,
creator of heaven and earth.

I believe in Jesus Christ, his only Son, our Lord,
who was conceived by the Holy Spirit,
born of the Virgin Mary,
suffered under Pontius Pilate,
was crucified, died, and was buried;
he descended to the dead.
On the third day he rose again;
he ascended into heaven,
he is seated at the right hand of the Father,
and he will come to judge the living and the dead.

I believe in the Holy Spirit,
the holy catholic Church,
the communion of saints,
the forgiveness of sins,
the resurrection of the body,
and the life everlasting.
Amen

The Magnificat (The Song of Mary) is said or sung

My soul proclaims the greatness of the Lord,
my spirit rejoices in God my Saviour;
he has looked with favour on his lowly servant.

From this day all generations will call me blessed;
the Almighty has done great things for me
and holy is his name.

He has mercy on those who fear him,
from generation to generation.

He has shown strength with his arm
and has scattered the proud in their conceit,

Casting down the mighty from their thrones
and lifting up the lowly.

He has filled the hungry with good things
and sent the rich away empty.

He has come to the aid of his servant Israel,
to remember his promise of mercy,

The promise made to our ancestors,
to Abraham and his children for ever.

Luke 1.46-55

The Gloria

Glory to the Father and to the Son:
and to the Holy Spirit;
as it was in the beginning is now:
and shall be for ever. Amen

or   Glory be to the Father and to the Son;
and to the Holy Spirit;
as it was in the beginning, is now, and ever shall be:
world without end. Amen

The Grace

The grace of our Lord Jesus Christ,
and the love of God,
and the fellowship of the Holy Spirit,
be with us all evermore. Amen

Ways of Focussing in Worship

Be still and know that I am God (Psalm 46.10)

It is much easier to concentrate on the things of God and of our worship when we are part of a great festival service in a cathedral or parish church. It isn't quite so easy when we are trying to worship with our branch or before a diocesan meeting in a church hall with little heating! Or in a room with flip charts and the paraphernalia which accompany meetings today. Having a visible focus for our worship helps us to remove the distractions around us. Our eyes are drawn towards whatever has been placed as our focus, and with our eyes, our hearts and minds are drawn towards the God we have come to worship.

Focal points are therefore very important to us in our spiritual life. Some people create special places within their homes to focus on God, or to have the space in which to be still. Some have a corner in their own home that has a simple crucifix on the wall or a candle burning. Here they can spend their quiet time each day.

We know that we can worship God wherever we are, but when we create a focus or a special atmosphere, we enhance our worship, whether in private or together with others. We create a sacred space and therefore, create sacred moments.

If we are leading public worship we need to be clear in our minds about what we are wanting to achieve, and our worship must always be welcoming - all must feel part of what is taking place. If people feel excluded by our type of worship, then we need to reconsider our original purpose.

Here is a simple checklist of ideas and objects you can use, in creating a sacred atmosphere in your daily and group worship.

* A simple cross on a table where all can see, with maybe the addition of a vase of flowers or a plant – something from nature quickly draws our minds to the Creator.

* A single candle, or a tray with small tea-lights, focuses us on the Light of the World.

* An icon, a picture, a piece of sculpture, large enough for all to see, which feeds our thoughts and prayers and allows us to experience the wonder of God's great love for each of us eg. Holman Hunt's 'The Light of the World', Salvador Dali's 'Christ of St John of the Cross' or other local images or objects that speak powerfully to our communities.

* A swathe of soft material which frames or gives a background to any of the above ideas. Material has the great effect of gathering together different items, of drawing the eye away from the world and directing us to the one we worship.

* A 'holding cross' shaped to fit into the palm of our hand as we pray, that again reminds us of Christ's great love for us.

* A smooth stone, perhaps received during the worship which helps us to reflect on the creation and on our own Christian witness as the 'living stones' in Christ's Church today.

* A bowl of water with petals or candles floating gently on it can help us to become calm and still our bodies.

* Anything from nature or our local culture and community – flowers, plants, the bough of a tree in bud, or traditional symbols of food or objects, – anything which allows us to praise God for his creation and helps us to reflect on God's unconditional love for every one of us.

* Some quiet music settles the hearts and minds and draws us into God's presence.

These are just some ideas – don't try to use all of them in one act of worship, but it is possible to combine some aspects to fit a particular theme. This is just a starting point.

You are created in the image of God, so whether you know it or not, you have something of the Creator within you. As you create your branch service, your deanery festival or other event – you are part of Creation. Praise God for that!

Prayer Resources

Suggested Marriage Service readings

For Marriage Services, renewal of marriage vows or celebrating various years of marriage, the following Scripture can be used:

WORD OF GOD

Suggested readings: Genesis 1: 26-28 + 31a; Psalm 128; Matthew 7:21+ 24-27; Mark 10: 6-9; Luke 24: 13-35; John 2:1-11; John 15:9-12; Romans 12: 1-2 + 9-13; 1 Cor 13; Eph 3:14; Eph 5:21-end; Col 3:12-17; John 4: 7-12

Where to go for help:

Collects and prayers for all seasons and occasions can be found in **Common Worship**, The **Book of Common Prayer** and other authorised service books of the Anglican Communion.

The Spirituality pages on our website: www.themothersunion.org include all our up-to-date prayers and resources. You will find our monthly midday prayers; prayers responding to crises in the news; worldwide prayers written by members from different countries; a list of all the resource books held in stock at Mary Sumner House; reflective and topical material; downloadable leaflets and other spiritual resources.

Useful website addresses

www.themothersunion.org

www.cofe.anglican.org/

www.un.org/events/calendar/calendar.htm

www.communigate.co.uk/ne/dailyprayer

www.worlddayofprayer.net

www.taize.fr then click on English for Taize Community

www.iona.org.uk then click on Liturgy Gander for
Wild Goose Resource Group

www.christian-aid.org.uk then click on Worship for
Christian Aid Society

www.natsoc.org.uk then click on Collective Worship for the
National Society

Other Prayer & Spirituality resources

Children in Church leaflets; Anthology of Public Prayer; Worship
book (now out of print); God's Story, Our Story; I belong to God,
Prayer Diary and Worldwide Voices. Various prayer cards are
also available.

Forthcoming publications will be listed on our website.

Acknowledgements

We are very grateful indeed to Sarah James, editor of the
Mothers' Union Worship Book. Her kind permission to use various
prayers and services from the Worship Book, many of which she
is the author, has been invaluable to us throughout this Book. We
are also very grateful to members' contributions from around the
world and the work of the Prayer and Spirituality Unit Committee.
Extracts from *Common Worship: Services and Prayers for the
Church of England* (Church House Publishing, 2000) are copyright
© The Archbishops' Council, 2000 and are reproduced with
permission.

Permission to photocopy

Material in this book, where the copyright is held by the Mothers'
Union, may be reproduced for local use, provided that such
material is not sold and that *Mothers' Union – United in Prayer &
Worship* is acknowledged as the source.